T0388699

WORMHOLES
EXPLAINED

THE
MYSTERIES
OF
SPACE

WORMHOLES
EXPLAINED

RICHARD GAUGHAN

Enslow Publishing
101 W. 23rd Street
Suite 240
New York, NY 10011
USA

enslow.com

For Adrienne, to let her know about wormholes that won't help her garden grow

Acknowledgements
Thanks to Stephanie Selman for poking holes where they needed to be poked, and to the staff at the Coconino County and Cline Libraries for helping ensure access to quality information.

Published in 2019 by Enslow Publishing, LLC.
101 W. 23rd Street, Suite 240, New York, NY 10011

Copyright © 2019 by Enslow Publishing, LLC.
All rights reserved.

No part of this book may be reproduced by any means without the written permission of the publisher.

Library of Congress Cataloging-in-Publication Data

Names: Gaughan, Richard, author.
Title: Wormholes explained / Richard Gaughan.
Description: New York : Enslow Publishing, [2019] | Series: The mysteries of space | Audience: Grades 7 to 12. | Includes bibliographical references and index.
Identifiers: LCCN 2017056154| ISBN 9780766099654 (library bound) | ISBN 9780766099661 (pbk.)
Subjects: LCSH: Wormholes (Physics)—Juvenile literature. | Space and time—Juvenile literature. | Cosmology—Juvenile literature. | General relativity (Physics)—Juvenile literature.
Classification: LCC QC173.6 .G38 2018 | DDC 523.1—dc23
LC record available at https://lccn.loc.gov/2017056154

Printed in the United States of America

To Our Readers: We have done our best to make sure all website addresses in this book were active and appropriate when we went to press. However, the author and the publisher have no control over and assume no liability for the material available on those websites or on any websites they may link to. Any comments or suggestions can be sent by email to customerservice@enslow.com.

Photos Credits: Cover Rost9/Shutterstock.com; pp. 6-7 Jurik Peter/Shutterstock.com; p. 8 Education Images/Universal Images Group/Getty Images; p. 11 The Protected Art Archive /Alamy Stock Photo; p. 13 © Paramount Television/courtesy Everett Collection; p. 17 AF archive /Alamy Stock Photo; pp. 20-21 Hulton Archive/Getty Images; pp. 23, 27 udaix/Shutterstock.com; pp. 24-25 posteriori/Shutterstock.com; p. 31 Nicky Rhodes/Shutterstock.com; p. 34 PM Images/Iconica/Getty Images; p. 37 Yellow Cat/Shutterstock.com; p. 38 Maxim Ahramenko /Shutterstock.com; p. 39 PeterVrabel/Shutterstock.com; pp. 40, 65 Rost9/Shutterstock.com; p. 43 Bettmann/Getty Images; p. 45 adapted from a diagram provided by the author; p. 48 wavebreakmedia/Shutterstock.com; p. 50 John T Takai/Shutterstock.com; p. 56 muratart /Shutterstock.com; p. 57 David A. Hardy/Science Source; p. 58 Mark Garlick/Science Photo Library /Getty Images; p. 63 Yurkoman/Shutterstock.com; p. 66 Yannick Mellier/IAP/Science Source; p. 68 snapgalleria/Shutterstock.com; back cover and interior pages sdecoret/Shutterstock.com (earth's atmosphere from space), clearviewstock/Shutterstock.com (space and stars).

CONTENTS

INTRODUCTION

Wormholes are something like "fairy godmothers": wormholes and fairy godmothers can both be useful, but no one has ever seen either one. There is an important difference, though; there is no evidence that fairy godmothers will be making midnight visits to prepare youngsters for the royal dance, while there is some reason to think that wormholes might be out there, waiting to be discovered. It's an exciting idea because the features of a wormhole would come in handy.

A wormhole connects distant places in the universe. It could even be a connection between this universe and another. A wormhole is different from anything else, but one way to think of it is as a tunnel that connects two sides of a mountain. Before the tunnel is built, the only way to get from one side to the other would be to climb up and down, or go a long way around. Then the tunnel goes in. Now the opposite side can be reached in just moments instead of taking all day.

Similar to the way in which a tunnel can shorten the trip between two sides of a mountain, a wormhole could be a shortcut across the universe.

One more feature of wormholes is similar to the tunnel through the mountains: the tunnel could be intentionally built, but it's also possible that a natural cave could connect the two sides. In the same way, the rules of physics don't care if a wormhole is built intentionally or if it exists naturally. Still, just like a cave *could* exist or a tunnel *could* be built, that doesn't mean it's there.

So why are there books, movies, and television shows about something that has never been seen?

Measurements from Earth indicate that Proxima Centauri (*center*) has an Earthlike planet (*right*) orbiting around it, but getting there to see it in person would take thousands of years—unless there's a working wormhole on hand!

The closest star to our solar system is Proxima Centauri. It's 4.2 light-years away—that's 25 trillion miles (40 trillion kilometers). According to the *Guinness Book of World Records*, the fastest human-made object was the *Helios 2* spacecraft, launched in 1976. *Helios 2* reached a top speed of 153,454 miles (246,960 km) per hour.[1] At that speed, it would take more than eighteen thousand years for *Helios 2* to reach Proxima Centauri.

Now imagine astronomers discover a wormhole entrance between the orbit of Mars and Jupiter. This imaginary wormhole makes a tunnel that cuts through to Proxima Centauri. The "tunnel" could trim the apparent distance down to 27 miles (43 kilometers). That's reachable in one day's travel—at walking speed! If wormholes exist, and if they are accessible, the universe changes from a vast desert with oases scattered here and there into a tiny playground full of children.

That's a thrilling prospect, worth being part of many stories.

But the belief in wormholes is based on more than just fanciful imagination. There's science to back it up. Albert Einstein came up with a very powerful theory called general relativity.

To understand why scientists believe wormholes could exist, one needs to understand a few things:

- the theory that describes gravity
- how scientists come up with theories
- why they use math in theories
- what it takes for scientists to trust any theory
- why they trust the theory that describes gravity

Then one can look at the big questions: can wormholes be real, and what would it take to travel through one of those tunnels all the way across the universe?

Chapter One

Wormholes in the Imagination

Wormholes—if they exist—make it possible to zip across gigantic distances. To a director who wants to make a movie or an author who wants to write a book, this makes things interesting. Without wormholes, a story about traveling from Earth to Proxima Centauri could be boring. An astronaut could climb on the most powerful rocket ever made and then get old and die before he or she even makes it one-hundredth of the way there.

Many books (and some movies) have been made about that kind of long travel, but they usually become stories about life on the ship. To make a story about what happens when voyagers make it to another planet, writers need shortcuts. They need wormholes.

Traveling Through *A Wrinkle in Time*

In Madeleine L'Engle's 1962 novel *A Wrinkle in Time*, Meg Murry and her companions flit from planet to planet. Meg is whisked

A *Wrinkle in Time* is one of many books (and movies) that uses a wormhole-like shortcut to have characters zip between worlds.

from a haunted farmhouse in Connecticut to a planet orbiting a star in Orion's belt. She is then carried even further across the universe to the imaginary planet Camazotz.[1]

The travelers don't take a starship. They don't even get in a bus, a train, or a car. Meg is shoved through something that feels like a plate of glass. Then she is on another planet.

How do Meg and her friends cross millions of miles in just a step or two? Meg gets an explanation. Imagine, she is told, that an insect walks from one edge of a cloth to another. It could take a long time. When the cloth is folded in half, though, the bug can get all the way from one end of the cloth to the other in a single step. The shortcut is like a "wrinkle" in the fabric. That's one way of describing the shortcut possible through a wormhole.

A Wrinkle in Time isn't the only fictional place where wormholes appear.

Spending the Day at the *Deep Space 9* Space Station

Wormholes are also very important in the television show *Star Trek: Deep Space 9* (1993–1999). During its 176-episode run on TV, the Deep Space 9 space station stood guard outside a wormhole.[2] The wormhole here exists naturally in the universe— no one built it. In this show, the wormhole is something like the on-ramp of a freeway with only two entrances.

Imagine, for example, that there were two ways to get from New York to Los Angeles. One way was to drive the 2,790 miles (4,490 km) of freeway between the two cities. The other was to drive 68 miles (110 km) from New York to Danbury, Connecticut, and enter a tunnel. A 6-mile (10-km) drive through the tunnel

The space station in the *Deep Space 9* television program offers services to space travelers the way that gas stations, restaurants, and hotels offer services to travelers on interstate highways.

would exit at Agua Dulce, California. Then only 43.5 miles (70 km) remain to get to Los Angeles. The freeway would take about a week to drive, while the tunnel trip would take less than a day.

If that tunnel really did exist, the two small cities at either end—Danbury and Agua Dulce—would become more important. Most people who wanted to go between Los Angeles and New York would choose the shortcut. They might want to have dinner, go shopping, or even stay overnight in Danbury or Agua Dulce before they start their trips.

That's what the *Deep Space 9* television show imagines would happen around a naturally occurring wormhole. The space station has restaurants, shops, and places to stay. All of that exists in the television show because of the wormhole tunnel across the galaxy.

Making *Contact* with Aliens

In the movie *Contact,* there is also a wormhole, but this one is constructed.[3] In fact, most of the movie is spent describing how the blueprint for the wormhole was discovered. The idea in *Contact* is that an alien civilization has realized that Earth is home to thinking creatures. The aliens have detected radio and television transmissions from broadcasts beginning in the early 1900s. The aliens think some creature on Earth might be capable of receiving and understanding a message. The aliens send a radio message to Earth. To be sure the Earth creatures are thinking, rational beings, they make the message very complex. The astronomers who detect the message can't just listen to it like a telephone call; they have to interpret pieces in the message like a puzzle with many layers.

SCIENCE FICTION ON THE EDGE

Science fiction is a genre that constructs stories of what might be. It depends upon imagination, but it's also limited. In fantasy, for example, writers can choose to have anything happen, such as having people transform into wolves. In realistic fiction, characters do everyday things such as end up running late for volleyball practice. Science fiction is in between. Unusual things happen, but they are unusual things that *could* happen if new discoveries are made or new inventions are developed.

That's why science fiction writers face a challenge if they want to write about spaceships or messages traveling the universe. Stars are a long way apart, so writers needed to have a way for their characters to take shortcuts. Wormholes are just what they're looking for.

Ellie Arroway (played by Jodie Foster) leads a team of astronomers who discover that the radio message contains the plans to build a giant machine. The machine has four huge rotating rings and a small capsule. Arroway hops in the capsule and travels in the machine. In a blaze of blinding energy, she enters a wormhole.

The wormhole takes Arroway to a distant star. The first wormhole has dropped her next to the entrance of another, which is connected to yet another. Her capsule hops from one wormhole to the next as if she is connecting from one highway to another, all the way across the universe. Presumably some alien creatures had built that entire network of wormholes.

Going on an *Interstellar* Journey

A wormhole is also very important to the story in the 2014 movie *Interstellar*.[4] The movie starts with Earth in a pretty bad situation: the air is bad and plants are diseased, and it's not looking good for the survival of humanity. But a wormhole has just appeared next to Saturn. The wormhole leads somewhere else in the universe—a space containing twelve planets that might be habitable. That is, people might be able to survive on one or more of those twelve planets. In the movie, the National Aeronautics and Space Administration (NASA) is still working hard to explore space and understand the universe. Part of that job is sending twelve different spaceships through the wormhole to explore. Before they can report back, though, things get so bad on Earth that the next ship needs to take off with enough supplies to start a new human colony on whichever of the twelve planets ends up being the nicest.

In the world of *Interstellar,* Joe Cooper (portrayed by Matthew McConaughey) is a farmer who used to be a NASA pilot. He gets to be in charge of the ship through the wormhole that's following after the twelve ships that went through together. He has some adventures and then makes a discovery: the wormhole that had appeared next to Saturn didn't just come out of nowhere, it had been built by people from the future.

The appearance of the wormhole in the movie *Interstellar* was designed with the help of leading scientists.

That sounds a little confusing, but wormholes are confusing things.

And they're also exciting, which is why they appear in so many books and movies. Of course, just because they are exciting does not mean they are real. Vampires and zombies can make for exciting books and movies, too, but they do not really exist.

Wormholes are different. No one has seen a wormhole, but they *might* exist. That raises an important question: no one has ever seen a zombie, but scientists know they don't exist. No one has ever seen a wormhole, but scientists say they could exist.

So what's the difference?

Chapter Two

Theories of Gravity

Although they've only been seen in movies and television shows, scientists predict wormholes can exist. They believe in the possibility of wormholes because they fit in with other things they understand and have observed. Those understandings are part of the theory of general relativity developed by Albert Einstein (1879–1955). The beginnings of that understanding lie in observations and calculations done hundreds of years ago, specifically in the year 1666.

Newton's Law of Universal Gravitation

In 1666, Isaac Newton (1643–1727) was a young Englishman who had just graduated from Cambridge University. He went home to his small village for a short vacation, but a deadly disease called the black plague was running wild in England. The only way the people at that time knew to fight it was to stay far away from one another. So the university was closed, and Newton was stuck home. To pass the time, he sat looking into his apple orchard for hours.[1]

Newton, sitting at his window, saw that apples always fall straight down, no matter how high the tree is. If a particular apple tree was ten times taller, he still expected the apple to fall straight to the ground. Even if an apple tree stretched all the way to the moon, he thought, the apple would still fall straight down . . . so doesn't it make sense that whatever makes the apple fall would also pull on the moon?

Those ideas led him to come up with one rule to describe the way objects fell, or, like the moon, didn't fall. He came up with a rule to describe the way different objects attract one another. He said the force of gravity between any two objects was proportional

Isaac Newton mused about the nature of gravity while watching apples fall from trees in the garden of his house.

to the mass of the two objects. That is, any two objects in the universe attract one another. A person standing on Earth, for example, is pulled toward the center of Earth. But the center of Earth is also pulled toward a person.

Newton's law of universal gravitation explains how Earth orbits the sun, how the moon orbits Earth, and how a soccer ball falls after it is kicked. Nearly every observation of gravity confirms that Newton was right.

Here's a way to think about Newton's idea: carefully set two marbles on a tabletop so they don't move. Now connect them with a rubber band. The rubber band pulls the marbles together. If you roll one of the marbles, it will pull the other along. With the right kind of push, the marbles could even end up spinning around one another. That's Newton's almost perfect model of how gravity works.

Almost perfect. Newton was mostly right, but his mathematical rule for describing gravity is a little off. Normally that doesn't make a difference. That is, Newton's law of universal gravitation is usually close enough that no one can tell that it's not perfect.

But sometimes it makes a big difference. For example, if an object is very heavy, then Newton's law doesn't quite describe what happens. Newton's law of universal gravitation needs to be tweaked a little to make it work perfectly.

Albert Einstein did the tweaking.

Einstein's General Relativity

Einstein started from a simple idea. He noticed that when a car accelerates, the driver feels as if she is pushed back in the seat. Now imagine all the windows in the car were blocked off. The driver of the car is pushed back into the seat. Can she say for

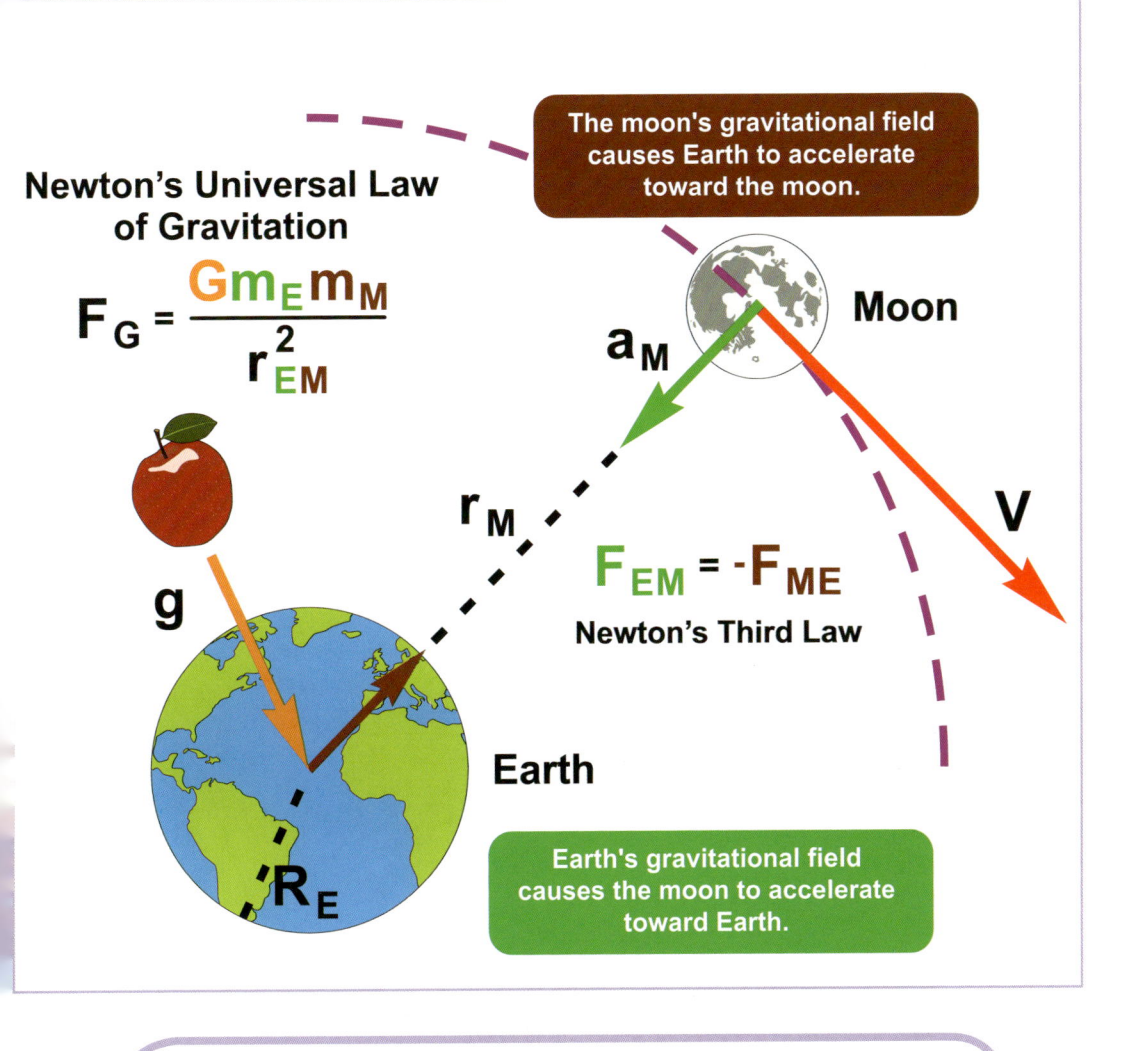

Newton's Universal Law of Gravitation

$$F_G = \frac{Gm_E m_M}{r_{EM}^2}$$

The moon's gravitational field causes Earth to accelerate toward the moon.

Moon

a_M

r_M

V

$F_{EM} = -F_{ME}$

Newton's Third Law

g

Earth

R_E

Earth's gravitational field causes the moon to accelerate toward Earth.

Newton's law of universal gravitation was the first scientific principle that connected motions in the heavens (like the moon's orbit) with observations on Earth (like apples falling). It states that the force of gravity (F_G) acting between any two objects (here, the moon [M] and Earth [E]) is directly proportional to the product of their masses ($m_E m_M$) and inversely proportional to the square of the distance between their centers (r_{EM}^2). The G represents Newton's gravitational constant.

certain that the car is accelerating? What if someone tilted the car up so that it was pointed straight into the sky? She would still feel as if she were being pushed back. How could she tell the difference?

Einstein said she couldn't. From that simple beginning, Einstein came up with a whole new understanding of how gravity

Where Newton's law said gravity was something like a rubber band connecting any two bodies, Einstein described gravity as the effect of masses on the shape of space itself, as illustrated below.

works. Einstein's mathematics are complicated to understand. But without the math, the ideas can be even tougher to grasp.

Here's Einstein's idea: imagine two marbles set on a tabletop, but this time, the top of the table is made of soft rubber. When the marbles are set down, they make little dimples in the rubber. This is an important difference between Newton's and Einstein's ideas. Newton imagined space was like a solid tabletop. Einstein said that space is kind of squishy and that it changes when marbles are put on top.

Because Einstein's table isn't flat any more, the marbles can move in the little dimples. If marble 1 is rolled close to marble 2, it won't travel in a straight line, but in a curve, following the edge of the depression caused by marble 2. Meanwhile, marble 2 will find itself rolling in the dimple caused by marble 1, so it will start to roll, too. The marbles don't do anything to one another, they only do things to the surface of the table. Then the curved surface of the table makes new paths on which the marbles can roll. That's Einstein's model for gravity, and it describes the world even better than Newton's model.

Newton's theory, as good as it is, is just a little off when describing the motion of the planets, what happens to satellites as they orbit Earth, and even the path that light follows as it travels the universe. Einstein's theory, which is known as general relativity, fixes those problems. Because Einstein's general relativity theory does such a good job of exactly describing those observations and more, scientists are very confident that general relativity is right.

UNDERSTANDING SPACE-TIME

Before Albert Einstein came up with his theory of general relativity, he came up with a different theory called the theory of special relativity. Imagine Jamahl and Germaine are sitting on their porches on opposite sides of the street. They both look at Max jogging down the street. Because they're on opposite sides of the street, Jamahl thinks the person is running right to left, while Germaine thinks the person is running left to right. But they both agree on the distance the person ran.

But if Jamahl is riding a *very* fast rocket as he goes by the street, things are different. The distance he measures will not be the same as Germaine's measurement! And when Jamahl and Germaine compare their measurements of the time Max starts

Einstein changed the way scientists understand the world by connecting the three dimensions of space with one more dimension: time. Together they make four-dimensional space-time. The cones in this diagram of space-time represent the locations in space and time that can influence or be influenced by this moment in the present, represented by the point at the junction of the cones. Time is up and down in the diagram, and the surface of the cones represent the travel of light in time and space. Anything outside the cones would have to be moving faster than the speed of light, and that's not possible, so only events within the past and future light cones can interact with this moment in the present.

and stops, they discover the times are also different. But when they make a calculation of time and distance together, their numbers agree again. That's because space and time are linked together into one thing called space-time.[2]

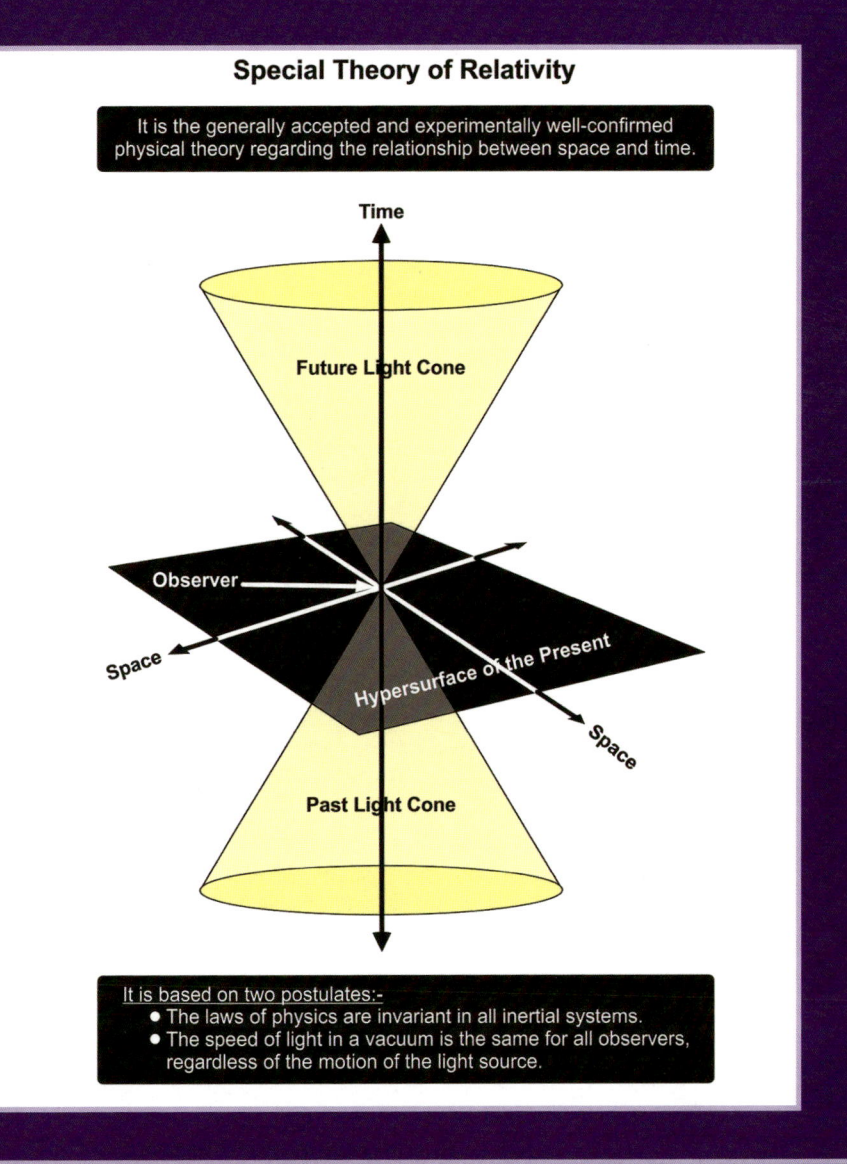

Special Theory of Relativity

It is the generally accepted and experimentally well-confirmed physical theory regarding the relationship between space and time.

Time

Future Light Cone

Observer

Space

Hypersurface of the Present

Space

Past Light Cone

It is based on two postulates:-
- The laws of physics are invariant in all inertial systems.
- The speed of light in a vacuum is the same for all observers, regardless of the motion of the light source.

Einstein did not make his predictions just by talking about how objects influence each other; he worked out ten equations. He put them together into one compact equation called Einstein's field equation.[3] Those equations are not as simple as adding up a grocery bill. Adding is a type of equation that has only one right answer. Einstein's equations have many different correct answers. In fact, even today, more than one hundred years after they were discovered, scientists are still trying to find solutions to Einstein's field equations.

Think back on the model of a marble on a squishy tabletop. Einstein's field equation says that the size and shape of the dimple on the tabletop is related to the mass of the marble. In fancier words (words that talk about the real world instead of a marble on a tabletop), the equation says something like "the curviness of space in a location is related to the heaviness of the objects at that location."

The Meaning of Einstein's Field Equation

The world is not a tabletop; so what does Einstein's field equation mean?

Our universe has three dimensions. If Ralph wants to meet Janice, he needs to know how far up the street he needs to walk, how far he should go after turning left or right, how much he needs to go upstairs or downstairs to get to Janice's office. Those three directions—forward/backward, left/right, and up/down—are called spatial coordinates. Ralph also needs one more piece of information to be sure he meets Janice: the time. Time is just that: the time coordinate. Put together spatial coordinates and time and you get something known as space-time.

Go back to the idea of marbles rolling on a tabletop. The tabletop has only two spatial dimensions because the marbles can't go up or down; they're on the table. It isn't too hard to imagine how marbles could squash down a soft tabletop or how their paths would change because the tabletop is curved. It's a little harder to imagine how four-dimensional space-time could get squished and curved, but general relativity says that's exactly what happens.

Time, space, and matter are mixed up together and squished around. Those are the first steps in the recipe for a wormhole.

What Is the Universe?

Science is an organized way of examining the world, so that's what scientists do: examine the world in an organized way. But what are they trying to do? What is the purpose of science?

The purpose is separate from the process. For example, weaving is a process of interlacing textile fibers so they hold together to create a sheet of fabric. That's the process, to put fibers together. The purpose is to produce a shirt or rug made of woven fiber material.

Science is a process of gathering information about the world and then figuring out the rules that describe how the world works. The purpose of science is to produce a mental model of some part of the universe.

For example, many frogs hibernate in winter and spawn in spring. Geraldo might discover that there are fewer frogs in spring after a long and cold winter. He might figure out that fewer frogs are hatched after cold winters because a particular molecule inside frog eggs is messed up if the mother frog is too cold when the eggs are growing inside her. Those observations and many other experiments could lead him to come up with a model that explains how different molecules work together to make an egg develop into a tadpole.

Experiments and observations help scientists devise models that demonstrate how frog eggs develop into tadpoles.

Sometimes it also works a little bit backward: models sometimes predict things that haven't been seen. For example, suppose Esperanza is also working with frog eggs, but she starts by calculating how a dozen different molecules in tadpole eggs *could* work together. Then—without knowing of any measurements—she uses her model to predict what would happen to the egg if there is a cold winter.

It happens both ways—sometimes the model is way ahead, making predictions about things that have never been seen; sometimes new measurements don't fit any existing model, so a whole new model needs to be generated. Most of the time, it's somewhere in the middle: some new measurements require a new model, then the new model predicts results that haven't yet been seen. The goal of science is not just to come up with an explanation for one single measurement. The goal is to come up with a model of the way the world works. Scientists call those models theories.

In most cases, theories are limited. Scientists who try to understand frog eggs don't need to worry about how the human eye reacts to light or what happens when atoms are squished by pressure so high they fall apart. Einstein's model of the universe, general relativity, is a model that tries to explain how the whole universe works.

General relativity is kind of like the foundation of a house. Scientists studying frog eggs or human vision or atoms under high pressure are working in rooms high up in that house. But everything they want to do is built on the foundation of that house. They can't do anything in their rooms that would make the foundation bend or crack. Those other scientists don't need to worry about the foundation of the house too much of the time, but if they plan to use some really heavy equipment they have to be concerned. In the same way, if scientists need to do anything that depends on how the world behaves around really heavy or really dense objects, then their work relies on general relativity.

That's why it's so important: at some level, everything depends upon general relativity.

What General Relativity Means

Einstein's theory of general relativity is a model that was pretty far ahead of the measurements. In fact, one hundred years later the model is still pretty far ahead of the measurements. Einstein did a lot of his experiments in his head. These *gedankenexperiments*, or "thought experiments," helped Einstein imagine the consequences of things he knew to be true.[1]

For example, one of the thought experiments Einstein considered was the one introduced in the previous chapter. Imagine Kristonya is sitting in a cushy spaceship with a nice reclining chair. The spaceship is coasting along, so she takes a nap. She wakes up and feels herself being pushed back into the chair. There are no windows, so she can't see where they are. How can she tell if the spaceship has landed or if the rockets are blasting away making the spaceship accelerate at exactly the acceleration of gravity on Earth?

Einstein added to that thought experiment. What if Kristonya happens to have darts? If she were on Earth and she threw the dart perfectly level across the cabin, it would hit the opposite wall lower than the height at which she threw it. That is, the dart would fall as it flies across the cabin. She tries the experiment and the dart lands at a lower spot on the wall than the height that she threw it. She figures she must be on Earth because the dart fell. Then she realizes that if she were in a spaceship that was speeding up, the dart would do the same thing. That's because the spaceship is speeding up all the time, including in the time between when the dart leaves her hand and when it hits the opposite wall. So when she let it go, it would be moving forward at the same speed as the rest of the ship, but after it leaves her hand, the spaceship speeds up a little more and moves ahead of

A dart thrown perfectly flat will hit a dartboard lower than the point at which it is released. That will happen if the dartboard is on Earth or in an accelerating spaceship.

the dart. The dart hits the opposite wall lower than the height at which she released it. The dart appears to have fallen. It behaves the same way whether she's in an accelerating spaceship or parked on the surface of Earth.

WEAK AND STRONG EQUIVALENCE PRINCIPLES

Einstein's general relativity says that any large or small mass can be thought of as a curvature in space-time. But the equations that describe how a soccer ball moves don't use that same definition of mass. That raises an important question: are the two types of mass the same? So far, all measurements have shown they are. That's called mass equivalence. It's also called the weak equivalence principle because there is another equivalence principle.

Einstein's thought experiment with the passenger in a spacecraft tests mass equivalence, but it tests more than that. It tests if there is *any* difference between the spaceship parked on the surface of Earth and a spaceship accelerating at that same rate. The idea that these are the same is called the strong equivalence principle, and it has also been tested frequently. So far, it appears to be true.[2]

Then Einstein added one more little bit to this thought experiment. What if, instead of throwing a dart, she fires light from a laser pointer? (There were no laser pointers in Einstein's time, so he imagined a flashlight.) If she is accelerating in a spaceship, the light will hit the opposite side just a little lower than the height from which she fires it. Would that happen if the spaceship was parked on Earth? Well, thought Einstein, the accelerating ship out in space and the parked ship on Earth are the same in every other way, so they must be the same in that way, too.[3]

Light must "fall down" on Earth. But light travels in straight lines! Einstein combined all those thoughts to come up with the idea that light travels as straight a line as it can. Think back on marbles rolling on a rubber table. The marbles roll in straight lines unless the rubber is pulled down to make a dimple. The marble rolls on the surface in as straight a line as it can, but the line is bent because the table itself is bent. So, said Einstein, light tries to travel in a straight line, but it can't because space itself is bent.[4]

What Does Space Look Like?

It's easy to imagine a rubber table that has little dimples in it. Unfortunately, it's much harder to imagine what the bent space around Earth looks like.

Here's the problem: imagine a drinking straw held far above a sheet of paper. When a light shines on the straw, there is a thin line of shadow on the paper. Imagine a creature that lives only in the line of shadow. It could crawl back and forth in the line. To describe its own motion, it could add a measurement of time, too. It could say something like, "At 3:22 I was 2.7 inches (6.8 centimeters) forward from the end of the world." That kind of world is one-dimensional because it has only one spatial dimension.

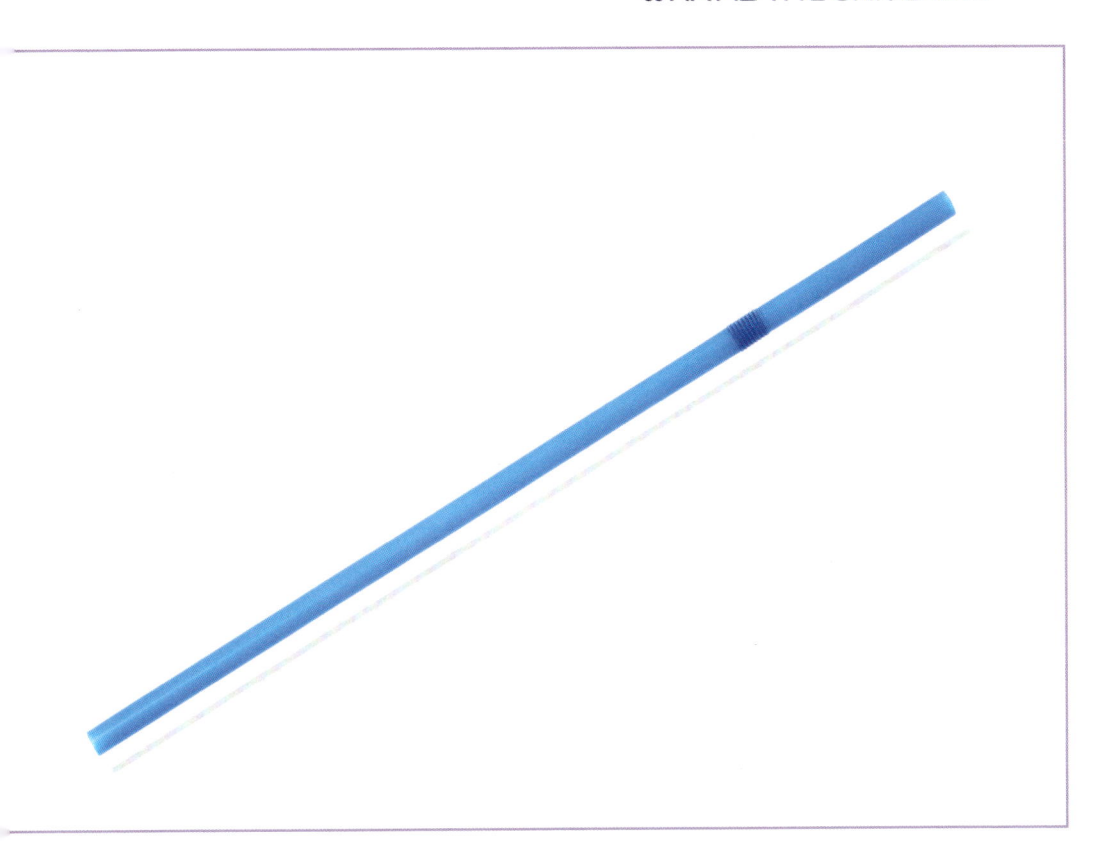

A creature that lived only in the shadow of this straw would only know how to move forward and backward and would not be aware that its shadow world was created from a larger world.

Now imagine the straw is brought closer to the paper so the shadow is wider, shaped like a rectangle. Creatures that live only in the world of that rectangular shape can move forward and backward, but they can also move left or right. One of these creatures could describe its own motion by saying something like, "At 9:13 I was 1.3 inches (3.4 centimeters) forward and 0.05 of an inch (0.12 of a centimeter) to the left from the edges of the world." That creature lives in a two-dimensional world because it has two spatial dimensions.

Any creature who lived in one of these shadows could travel forward and backward or left or right—movement along two different directions in that two-dimensional world.

One more strange world to imagine is the straw itself. Creatures who live in the straw universe can describe where they are by saying something like, "At high noon I was 5 inches (12.7 centimeters) forward, 0.08 of an inch (0.2 of a centimeter) left, and 0.1 of an inch (0.3 of a centimeter) up from the edge of the world." That's a three-dimensional world, like our universe.

Imagine a creature that lived in one of these straws. It could travel forward and backward, left and right, or up and down—three different ways to move in this three-dimensional universe.

What happens if the creatures from the two-dimensional world tried to describe their world to folks from the one-dimensional world? The one-dimensional creatures can only imagine movement in one direction, forward or back. When the two-dimensional creatures say, "Just turn left," the one-dimensional creatures can't even imagine what such a movement would look like.

The same thing happens when three-dimensional creatures talk with the two-dimensional folks. "Just go up 13 millimeters" they could say, and the two-dimensional people would say "What's 'up'?" And they wouldn't mean "what's happening," they would mean they have no idea what direction is "up."

Just as creatures living in a one- or two-dimensional world can't imagine a three-dimensional world, humans cannot truly imagine the higher-dimensional way in which space is curved. This visual of Earth and the sun bending the fabric of space-time around them is as close as it can come.

If people from a four-dimensional world tried to talk to creatures in a three-dimensional world, the three-dimensional creatures would have no way of understanding a completely new direction. The new direction wouldn't be up or down, left or right, or backward or forward. The three-dimensional creatures can only sense those directions, so they would have no clue what the new direction meant.

We live in a three-dimensional world and cannot visualize four spatial dimensions, and the "curving" that Einstein described is not in one of our three dimensions. That's why all the methods of describing the universe are tough to visualize. The purpose of science is to create mental models, and the purpose of Einstein's general relativity is to create a mental model of the universe. But the universe that Einstein described is almost impossible to visualize.

That's one reason Einstein described his theory using complicated mathematics. The structure of the universe is nearly impossible to visualize, but the mathematics that describe that structure can provide insight into how the universe works.

Chapter Four

Scientific Reasoning

Wormholes are very strange things. They are shortcuts connecting two parts of the universe. The only reason scientists believe wormholes could possibly exist is because they are a prediction of the mathematics of general relativity. It's reasonable to ask if mathematics can be trusted at all. How do scientists use mathematics? How do they decide *when* to trust the math?

The mathematician and computer scientist Richard Hamming (1915–1998) thought of mathematics as a tool for carrying out long chains of tight reasoning.[1] Think of the example of scientists investigating frog eggs. They are trying to understand how cold affects the spring spawn of frogs. They can only test their understanding if they can describe the situation with mathematics.

Imagine it is a cold winter and the scientists say, "Fewer frogs will be born because it's cold." Then only one-third as many frogs are born that year than in the warmer year before. They could *believe* they are right. But then they test the water and find

Richard Hamming (*right*) discusses computer technology with author Fred Gruenberger in 1962. Behind them is a flow chart of the logic program that goes into the computer. Like a program made up of sequential instructions computers use to perform a specific task, mathematical thinking allows very precise reasoning—one level of understanding built upon another and another—to provide specific answers to scientific questions.

high levels of laundry detergent residue. Now they don't know how much of the problem was caused by low temperatures and how much was due to pollution.

If, instead, they had a mathematical model, they would have a detailed prediction. Their model might say that if the lowest temperature was 22.1° F (-5.5° C), they would expect that only half as many frogs would hatch into tadpoles. When only one-third that many frogs are born, the scientists know something else must be going on—perhaps due to the pollution, and perhaps not. If the prediction of their theory matches the measurement, they would trust their theory and decide that maybe pollution doesn't make much difference.

That's what Hamming meant by "tight reasoning." Tight reasoning is needed for scientists to be able to tell if their mental models are correct. But more than that is needed. The even bigger question is "Why do we believe that the world works according to mathematical rules?"

Math and the World

There is a lot of philosophical discussion about how lucky it is that the world seems to work according to mathematical rules.[2] It is not as strange as it might seem. The important thing is that the world works according to any rules at all. As long as there is order and consistency to the universe, then it can be described by some sort of mathematics, even if it would be different from the mathematics taught in middle school.

For example, mathematics in school teaches that the three angles of a triangle add up to 180 degrees. That rule has been used to build bridges, and bridges generally don't fall down, so that rule works—but not in every situation. In fact, it doesn't even work on all of Earth. Imagine a triangle drawn on the surface of Earth. The first leg of the triangle starts at the equator and goes in a straight line right along the equator for about 6,214 miles (10,000 km). The next leg starts with a right angle, a 90-degree turn headed all the way to the North Pole. From the North Pole, there's *another* right-angle turn, then a line all the way back to

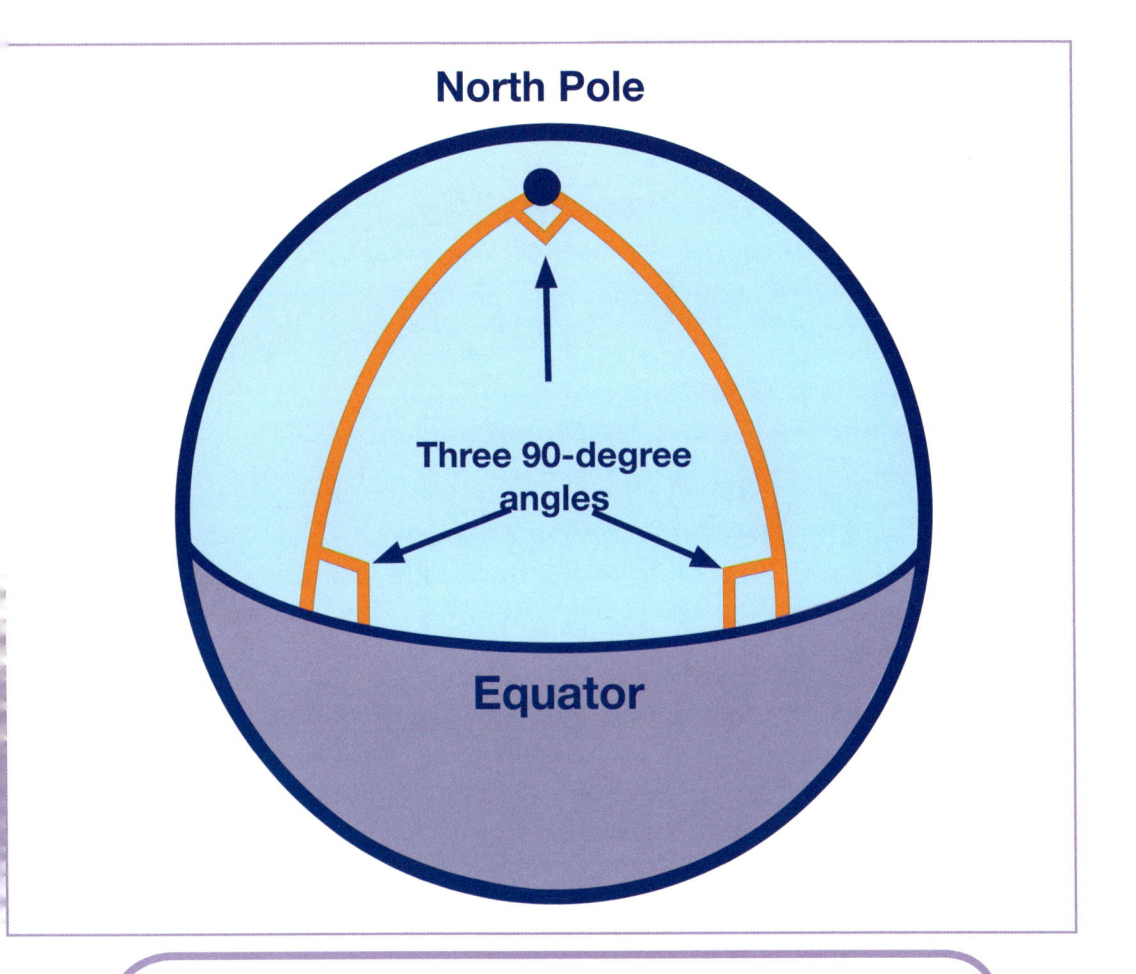

The three angles in a triangle drawn on a flat piece of paper always add up to 180 degrees. On a different surface, such as the spherical surface of Earth, that rule doesn't apply, but a more complicated version of that rule *does* work.

the starting point on the equator—where the two legs meet at even another right angle. The three right angles in that triangle add to 270 degrees!

This doesn't mean that math doesn't work; it means that scientists *make* math work by choosing the set of mathematical rules that match the way the world works. For building a highway or slicing a pie, junior high math works just fine. In other circumstances, the rules of math are tweaked just a little. It can get kind of complicated, but it's not as complicated as it sounds. The simple triangle theorems don't work for that giant triangle on the surface of Earth because Earth isn't flat. But there's a special, slightly more complicated form of the equations that work for curved surfaces, and those more complicated equations turn into the simple equations for a flat surface. That is, elementary school math is not wrong, it just doesn't describe everything. But there is other math that works for other situations.

When a bowling ball on Earth drops, it falls down hard every time. There's an equation for that. Frog eggs hatch according to an equation. Bacteria turn milk into cheese in a way described by an equation.

Math describes the world, so precise and accurate scientific models must use mathematics to describe the world.

Doubt and Certainty

There is one more piece of information needed before getting into the details of general relativity. It's important to understand the difference between doubt and certainty in science. When do scientists trust their mathematical theories? The line between doubt and certainty can be understood with another gedankenexperiment, another thought experiment.

NEW MATH

Mathematics describes reality. But what if it didn't? What if every time two things were added together, each of them became one and a half times bigger? In that strange world, every time two pennies were put together they would each turn one and a half times bigger. In that universe, one plus one would equal one and a half and one and a half. Strange as it is, a new kind of math could be invented that would match that universe. The rules of mathematics still apply. Addition could still be done in any order, and it could be undone with a special kind of subtraction. As long as the universe acts according to consistent rules, mathematics will be able to describe those rules. In fact, mathematics describes the universe more accurately than words alone can.

Imagine a box. It has something in it, something unknown. It's sealed and has no cracks or holes. Suppose Jane is given the job of figuring out what's inside the box. Jane could shake the box, smell the box, weigh the box. The only rule is that she can't open the box. Suppose the box rattles a little when it's shaken. Maybe it's a little heavy, but not too heavy to be easily picked up. Jane might make a test box: a physical model of what she thinks might be in the box. Perhaps she would fill it with rocks from the garden, or glass beads, or colored gravel from an aquarium. She would test her physical model and the unknown box. Do they

It's only natural to want to know what's inside a box. The work of science is like figuring out what's in the box *without being able to open it*!

weigh the same, sound the same, feel the same? Jane decides that the box is full of colored aquarium gravel.

But after she decides that, she learns that there are a couple other types of gravel. Some gravel is made to protect the soil around plants, some is made to decorate garden paths, and some is made to hold down empty pie crusts while they're being baked. She makes new model boxes with each of the new types of gravel, but all the boxes weigh about the same, sound about the same, and feel about the same. Then Jill comes by and asks what's in the box. Jane has to admit she doesn't really know. Jill tells her there's a baseball bat inside. Jane argues, but Jill reminds Jane that she just admitted she doesn't know what's in the box.

Jane is confused because Jill's right; she doesn't know what's in the box. But then she realizes that even though she isn't certain of what is in the box, she has a pretty good idea of what it *isn't*. It's not full of cotton balls or potato chips or raccoons—and it certainly isn't stuffed with a baseball bat. She knows because she has built a mental model of what's in the box, and her mental model fits the facts: the rattle, the weight, the feel. None of those other objects would match the evidence. So even though Jane still has some questions about the box, she knows a lot.

That's almost always the situation in science. Scientists always have questions. There are always things they don't know. But a tested theory is supported by evidence, so they have a good idea that it's mostly true. New things can always be learned, and sometimes theories need to be changed, but that doesn't mean the whole theory is wrong.

Scientists have never been to the middle of the sun, but they have gathered information that lets them develop a mental model of the reactions that drive the sun to produce energy.[3] They

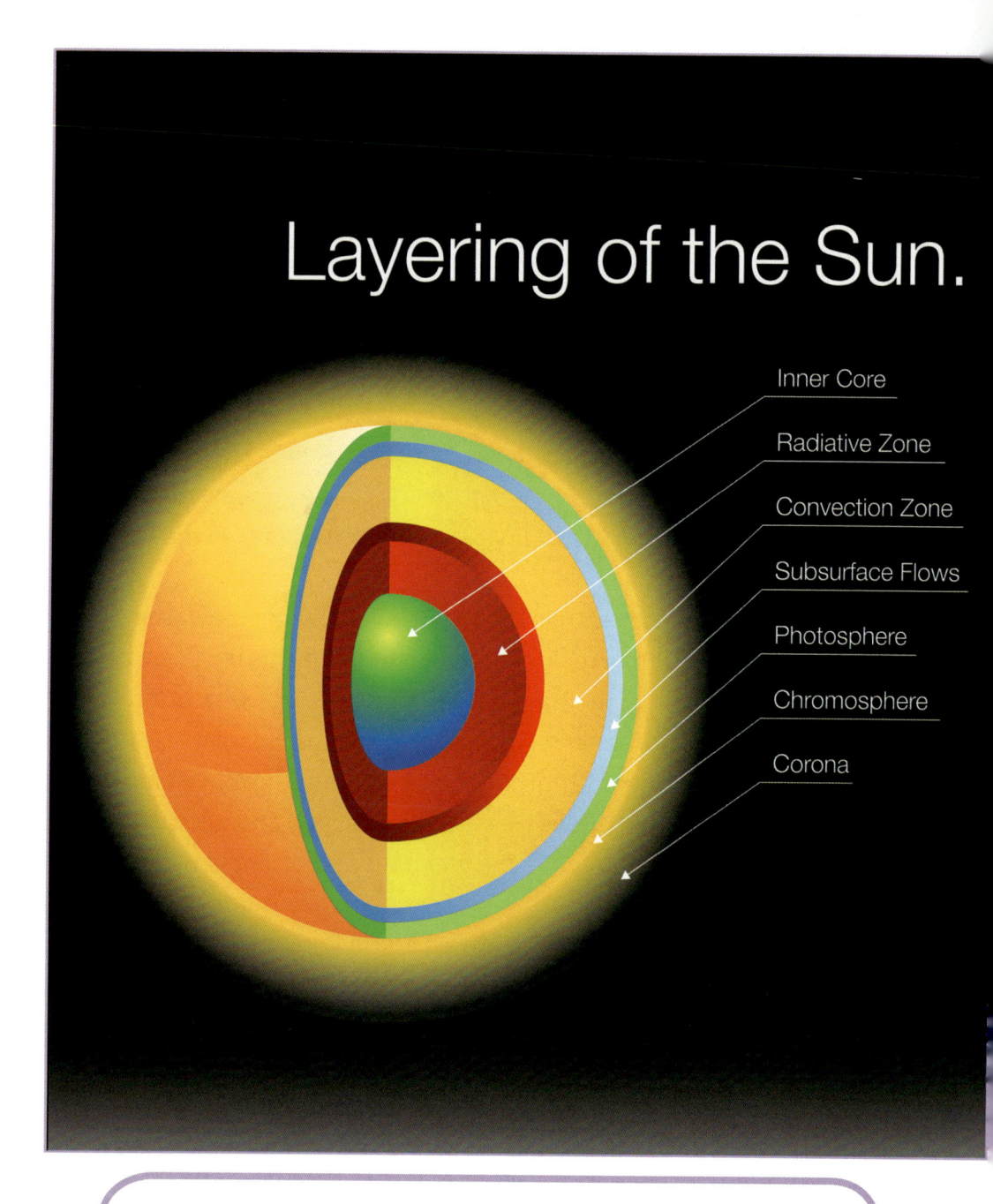

Layering of the Sun.

Inner Core

Radiative Zone

Convection Zone

Subsurface Flows

Photosphere

Chromosphere

Corona

Astronomical observations, experiments on Earth, and a mathematical model come together to provide scientists with a good theory of the internal workings of the sun.

describe their mental model with mathematics, then make very precise predictions about what they should measure. The more measurements match their predictions, the more confidence they have in their mathematical mental model. If their predictions were wrong, then they check their theory and see if they need to change their mental model.

General relativity makes some pretty strange predictions. In the hundred years or so since Einstein formulated his field equation, many of those predictions have been observed. Many more have not yet been seen—wormholes, for example, are predicted but not yet observed. Just like a box with a mystery object inside, scientists are sure about many aspects of general relativity. For other parts, questions still remain.

Chapter
Five

Proving General Relativity

Einstein's field equation is a mathematical model for the structure of the universe. The field equation is:

$$R_{\mu v} - \frac{1}{2} R g_{\mu v} + g_{\mu v} \Lambda = \frac{8\pi G}{c^4} T_{\mu v}$$

That's not a very long equation for describing the structure of the whole universe, but it's not an equation like 2 + 2 = 4. It is an expression that connects different things into a pattern.[1]

That same kind of equation can describe everyday activities. This one is an example:

$$\sum_{i=1}^{m} a_i * C_i \leq T(t)$$

An equation doesn't mean much without an understanding of the pieces that go into it. The Σ symbol at the beginning just means "start at the first item and add up all the separate things that follow." The a represents how many of item i are bought, while the C in that equation represents the cost for each item, starting from the first, which we label with $i=1$, going to the second, when $i=2$, and going all the way to the last item, the number m. If the shopper buys six items then m equals 6, and if the shopper buys 597 items then m equals 597. The next symbol, the sideways V with a bar under it means "is less than or equal to." The $T(t)$ represents the total amount of money a shopper has today. So that fancy equation says something like, "The total cost of everything that a shopper buys today is less than or equal to the amount of money the shopper has today."

The important thing about that equation is that it doesn't say anything about how much money the shopper has or how many products the shopper buys. If Jim has twelve dollars and buys four loaves of bread for three dollars each, then the equation is true. If Janae has one million dollars and buys a house for seven hundred fifty thousand and a cell phone for four hundred, the equation is true. In fact, no matter how many situations someone describes with that equation, there is always one more possibility. But it doesn't mean all those possibilities come true. Janae *could* buy one hundred million gumballs with her million dollars, but it's unlikely she would do that.

In Einstein's field equation, all those complicated looking R and g terms on the left hand side of the equals sign represent how space-time is "curved," and the terms on the right hand side represent how much "energy" is in a space. Einstein's more famous equation, $E = mc^2$, says that energy is equal to mass multiplied by a really big number. "Energy" in Einstein's field equation really means energy and mass (and a little bit of more complicated stuff). So Einstein's field equation says something like, "The way that space-time is curved depends upon how much energy and matter are around." The equation also says, "The more energy and matter are around, the more that space-time will be curved." As in the equation about what a shopper

TESTING THEORIES

Science is all about making mental models of the physical world. Those models are scientific theories, and the more evidence that supports them, the stronger they become. Scientists make hypotheses—predictions about how a measurement will come out—before they make observations or do experiments.[2] One of the reasons for making a hypothesis is so scientists can figure out if their theory is right or needs to be tweaked a little or needs to be replaced with an entirely new theory. If a theory has already been supported by lots of measurements, then scientists will do what they can to tweak it. For example, Newton's law of universal gravitation had been verified very well, so when scientists measured something unexpected in the orbit of the planet Mercury, they tried to fit it into Newton's theory. They guessed there might be another planet even closer to the sun.[3] That didn't make things work out, so the explanation for the behavior of gravity near a heavy object needed to wait for Einstein to figure it out.

can buy, Einstein's field equation has many solutions. Some of those solutions are pretty strange. So why do scientists believe Einstein's field equation is true?

Strange Predictions for Strange Behavior

In 1915, when Einstein came up with his theory of general relativity, astronomers already had a mystery they couldn't explain. The planet Mercury didn't move the way it was supposed to. Einstein examined his new theory and realized his equation predicted the already-observed motion of Mercury.

That was good, but that was for an effect scientists had already seen. Einstein's theory also predicted a few things that no one had ever seen.[4] For example, general relativity predicted that when observers on Earth looked at stars that passed behind the sun, the light from those stars would be bent by the curved space near the sun. That effect was impossible to measure because the sun's light was far too bright to allow astronomers to see stars lined up so close. But during an eclipse, light from the sun is blocked by the moon, which means those distant, dimmer stars can be seen. In 1919 there was such an eclipse, and the stars appeared to shift just as predicted by Einstein's equation. Since then, the effect has been measured and verified even more accurately by bouncing radar signals off of planets as they pass behind the sun.

Einstein predicted that clocks at high altitudes would appear to run faster than clocks at sea level.[5] That's a prediction no one would have imagined before Einstein's theory—but it was measured in 1976. The Global Positioning System (GPS) satellite system uses clocks and radio signals in space to figure out the position of a cell phone on Earth. GPS works only because it

A solar eclipse lets astronomers see light from stars that would normally be hidden by the brightness of the sun.

takes that time shift into account, so Einstein's strange prediction is verified millions of times every day.[6]

Einstein also predicted that light would change color as it travels from a "more curved" space-time to a "less curved" space-time. That is, light would get redder as it travels up from Earth's surface. That's the same effect that causes car horns to sound higher pitched as the car approaches and decrease in pitch as the car travels away. That's called the Doppler shift, and it normally only happens with moving objects. Einstein's theory

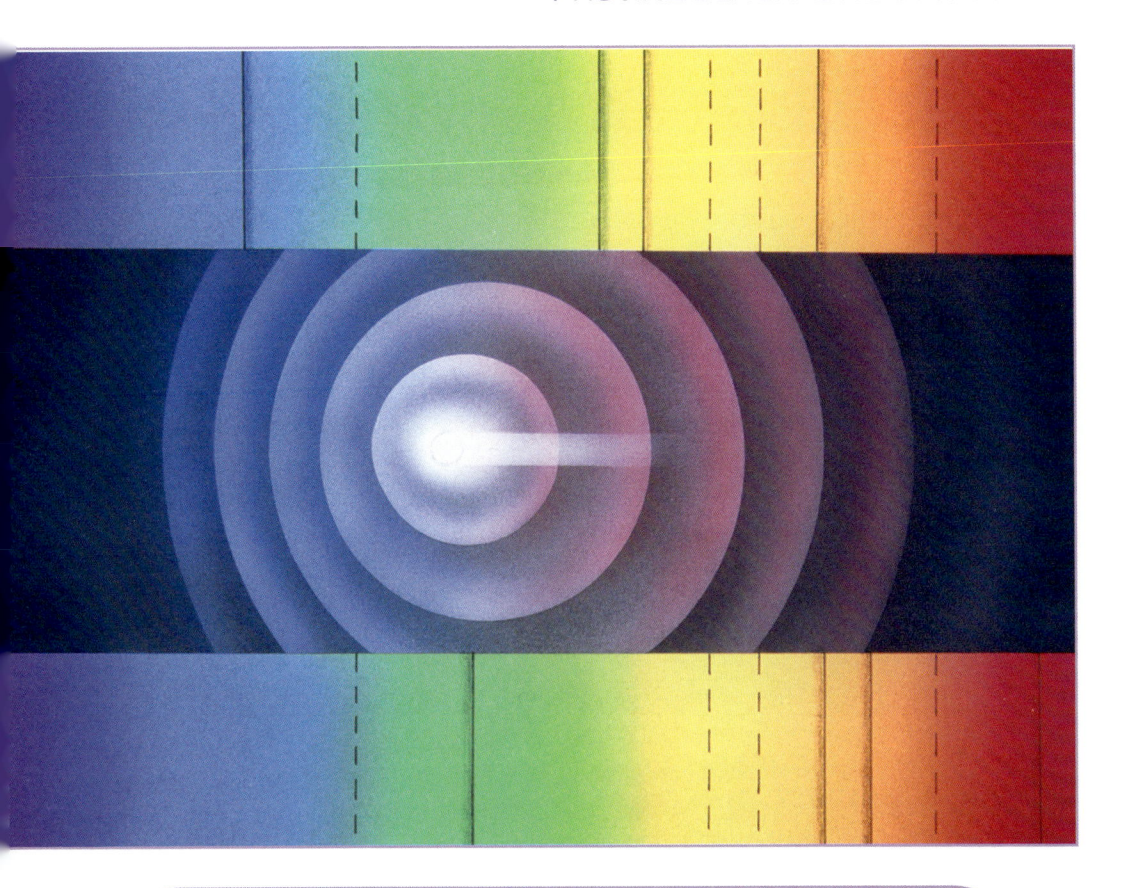

When an object (for example, this light in the center) moves away from an observer, the observer detects a decrease in the frequency of the energy it has emitted: sounds get lower pitched and light gets "redder." Einstein predicted the same thing would happen to light moving from a region of higher gravity to a region of lower gravity.

predicted it would happen with no motion, and—again—he was right. That effect was first accurately measured in 1960 and has since been measured even more accurately.[7]

Those predictions are all strange and impressive, but they each tested only a tiny part of Einstein's theory. In September of 2015, a pair of very sensitive 2.5-mile-long (4-km) sensors detected gravitational waves.[8] Gravitational waves would only exist if Einstein's theory was correct, and they have now been found. Similar to the way that sound waves are compressions and expansions in air, gravitational waves are stretches and compressions in the fabric of space-time. When a plate crashes to the floor in the kitchen of a restaurant, the people eating their

When very heavy objects move rapidly, they send vibrations through the fabric of space-time. Those vibrations are gravitational waves, and they have now been detected.

lunch in the dining room can tell whether it was a metal, plastic, or ceramic plate by the sound it makes. With two ears, they can even tell where the plate was dropped. Those same principles apply to the detection of gravitational waves. When something changes dramatically—such as two really heavy objects crashing together—a shiver goes through space-time. That shiver is a gravitational wave.

Einstein's theory predicted all those strange things, and all those strange things were discovered. Those and other observations are why scientists are confident that Einstein's theory is correct.

Wondering About Wormholes

Until 2015 gravitational waves were a prediction of general relativity that had not been verified. Today wormholes are in the same boat—they are a prediction that hasn't been verified. There is one big difference between the two predictions, though: the likelihood of the prediction being true.

Think back to the shopper equation. That equation will be true for all sorts of purchases, but they aren't all equally likely. For example, if Jim has three children, it's likely he'll buy bread at least once a week. Meanwhile, Janae, with her million dollars, is very unlikely to buy one hundred million gumballs.

Gravitational waves are a very likely solution to Einstein's equation. They are so likely that if they hadn't been found, scientists would question whether Einstein's equation was even true. Wormholes are an unlikely solution. They might be out there, but only if very strange conditions are met.

Remember the rubber table that gives a way to think about space-time? The surface of that rubber table gets "dimpled" when marbles are sitting on it. The heavier the marble (or the larger its energy), the bigger the dimple. That dimple represents the way that space is curved. In Einstein's theory, that is called the curvature of space-time. At some point, when the energy in a small spot gets very high, the curvature becomes so large—the dimple gets so stretched—that space-time "breaks." The dimple in the rubber table breaks through, making a little hole in the surface.

That little hole could be the seed of a wormhole, the opening of a gate to a different space.

Chapter Six

Through the Wormhole

One more bit of mathematics needs to be taken care of to prepare to travel through the wormhole. It turns out that Einstein's field equation could be part of a bigger theory. In fact, scientists really hope that it is because they believe that all the forces in the universe are just different ways of looking at the same force.

Think of a flash of lightning. It's bright, which is a flash of light. It's loud when the thunder rolls. It's full of electrical energy that can fry anything it hits. All three of those things are different, but they all come from the same source. That's kind of like what scientists expect to discover: a way of understanding electricity, gravity, and other forces as just different aspects of some other force that has not yet been discovered.

Even though scientists don't know what that other force would be, they have some ideas about what it would have to look like. One of the most surprising things is that the three-dimensional universe of Earth must be part of a universe with more dimensions.[1] Think back to the example of creatures that live in a one-dimensional universe, a universe that was just the shadow of a three-dimensional straw. In the same way as those creatures live in a universe that is a flattened shadow of a three-dimensional universe, Earth's universe is a shadow of a higher-dimensional universe. It's a hard thing to imagine.

Now try something even harder: think of the three-dimensional universe like a sheet of paper. The idea that this universe is part of a higher dimensional universe can be thought of as if that piece of paper is floating around in a bathtub. Living in the sheet-of-paper universe we have no way of knowing the universe is floating in an entirely other space because our entire universe — our whole space-time — is contained within that sheet of paper.[2]

Now recall that general relativity predicts that very heavy objects create holes in space-time. In 1935 Albert Einstein and physicist Nathan Rosen (1909–1995) were trying to "patch the holes." They discovered that it was mathematically possible to skip right over the hole in space-time.[3] The mathematics they worked out allows an object to approach the hole in space-time in one location and slip around to another location in space-time. The theory doesn't put any limitations on the other location. They called this a "bridge" and not a wormhole, but it's the same thing. If the entrance to the wormhole is in one spot in that piece of paper in the bathtub, the exit can be anywhere else in the paper. It's kind of like the sheet of paper is curled around in the water and the wormhole is a little string connecting one spot on the paper to another spot somewhere else on the paper.

There's one problem with the Einstein-Rosen bridge. As soon as something tries to go through it, it will collapse. That is an unstable wormhole. All is not lost, though, because Einstein's field equations also allow stable wormholes to exist.

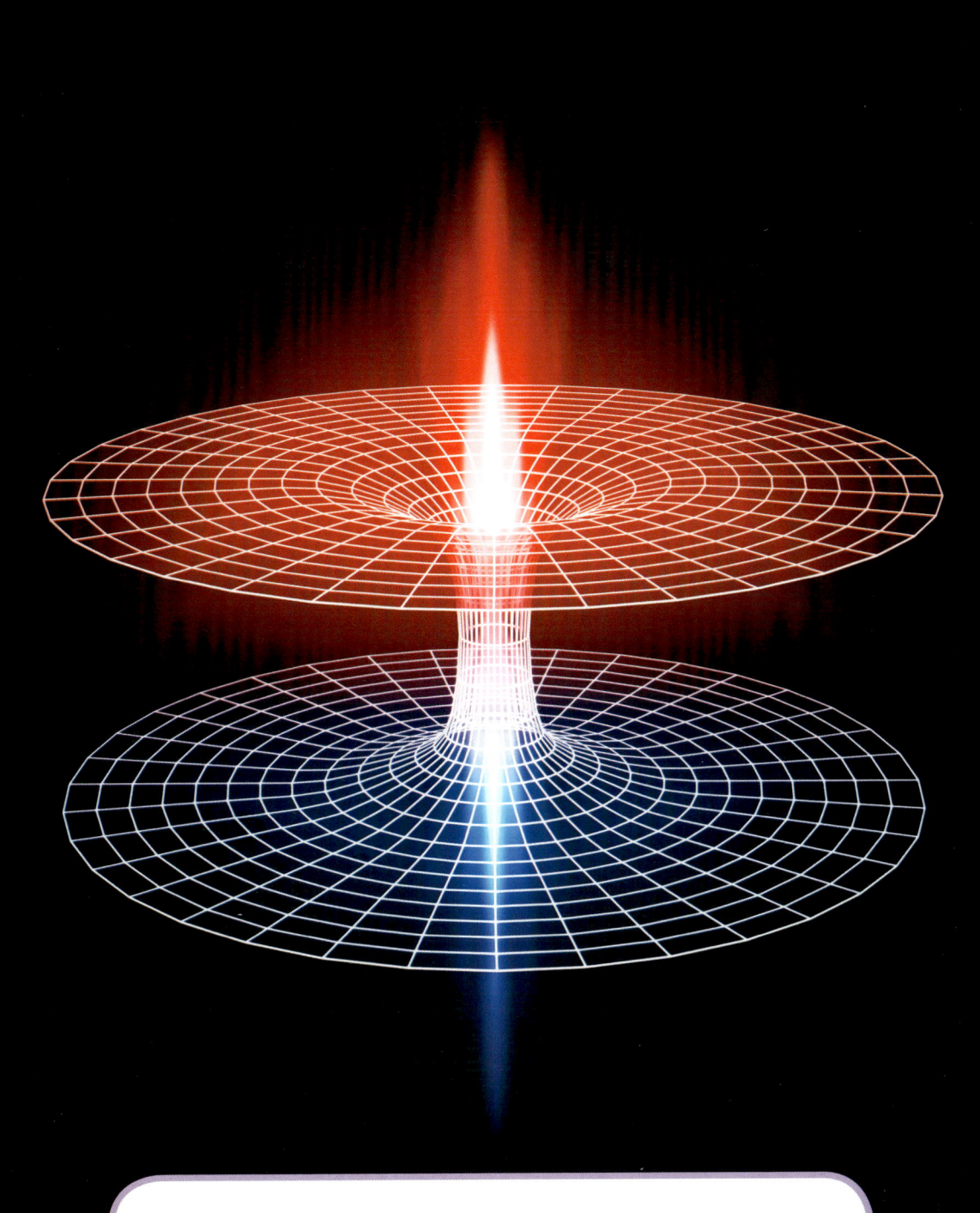

Very dense matter can curve space-time so strongly that it "tears," possibly making a connection to a different part of the universe—an Einstein-Rosen bridge.

Traversable Wormholes

Most of the possible solutions to Einstein's field equation have not yet been discovered, but there are partial solutions for some special cases. So even without full solutions, scientists can classify the types of wormholes. Solutions have been worked out for heavy spinning objects. A heavy spinning mass—a kind of donut ring of very dense matter—for example, can create a stable Kerr wormhole. Charged wormholes can also be stable. So wormholes can be spinning or not, charged or uncharged, microscopic or large. Wormholes can also connect different types of places.

Remember the sheet-of-paper universe in the bathtub? There's nothing to say that there can't be more than one sheet of paper floating in the tub. The universes are separate, and people in one universe would not be aware that any other universes existed. But there's nothing to keep a wormhole in one universe from connecting to another universe.

Traversable wormholes are broken places in space-time where information can theoretically go from one location to another spot somewhere else in this universe or perhaps even a different universe.[4] But the objects that create wormholes are so heavy that anyone passing close would be stretched into long, thin shapes, a process called spaghettification. And there's one other problem: keeping a traversable wormhole open would require a whole lot of energy and matter.

The equations of general relativity have led here. There could be big and small wormholes, spinning and stationary wormholes, charged and uncharged wormholes, wormholes connecting spots in this universe, and wormholes that connect spots between different universes. All of those are possible, but

Matter that is dense enough to create a wormhole is also dense enough to stretch and pull apart anything that gets too close.

so far none of them have been found. One reason they haven't been found might be because they require very large collections of matter and energy. So even though they *might* exist, they might not.

But one hope remains. Something else no one has ever seen: exotic matter.[5]

What It Would Take

If someone could travel through a wormhole, they would be able to zip across the universe in moments or even jet across from one universe to another. So it sure would be nice to be able to build a wormhole that was large and stable and wouldn't crush people who traveled through. The hope lies in strange forms of matter and energy: dark matter and dark energy, and even negative energy.[6] Dark matter and dark energy do not interact with other objects in

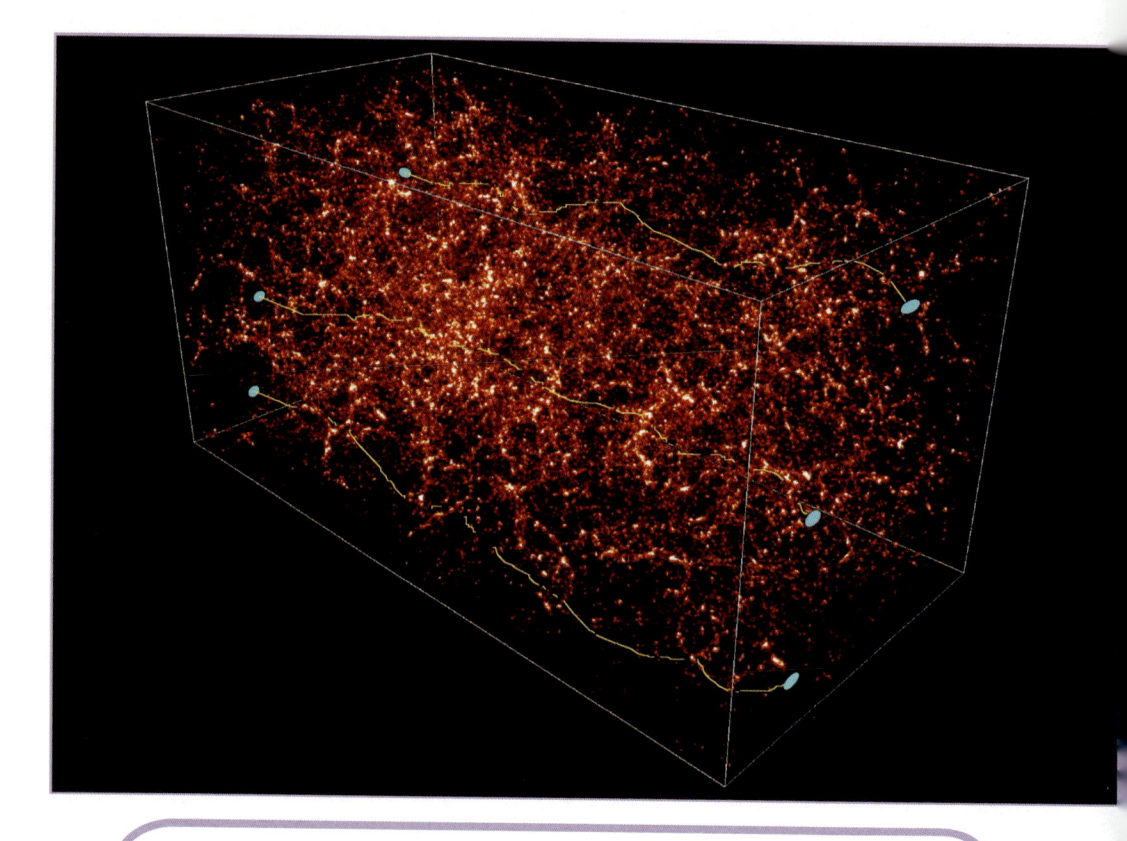

Astronomical observations have convinced scientists that the universe is filled with dark matter, shown in red in this map of a portion of the universe. The blue ovals are galaxies and the yellow lines are their light being pulled by dark matter.

the same way ordinary matter and energy interact. Astronomical observations show that dark matter and dark energy must exist, but scientists know almost nothing about them. So far, negative energy has only been found in very small amounts. If it could be controlled, though, negative energy—along with dark matter and dark energy—may be the key to opening a traversable wormhole and keeping it open.

NEGATIVE ENERGY

There are two parts to the energy of a particle. One part is called the rest energy, and it is always positive. The part of the energy that's due to movement is also always positive. So how can energy be negative? One strange measurement gives a hint of how it can be done.

It turns out that all of space is filled with energy. When two mirrors are put very close to one another, they block some of that energy from the space between the mirrors.[7] That space has a negative energy compared to the energy filling even empty space. Scientists have no idea how that negative energy could be harnessed.

Along with negative energy, dark matter and dark energy could also help maintain a black hole. Although astronomical measurements indicate dark matter and dark energy are out there, scientists have very little idea what they would look like—but something unusual is needed to make a traversable wormhole, and dark matter and energy are strange!

There's one more hope. Einstein's theory of general relativity is very good, but it's not perfect. For example, general relativity says that space will be curved even by the smallest bits of matter, things such as molecules, atoms, and protons. But the equations of general relativity don't match up with the predictions of the very successful theory that describes how such small particles act. So general relativity will have to be modified, and it will have to be modified at the small scales of dark matter, dark energy,

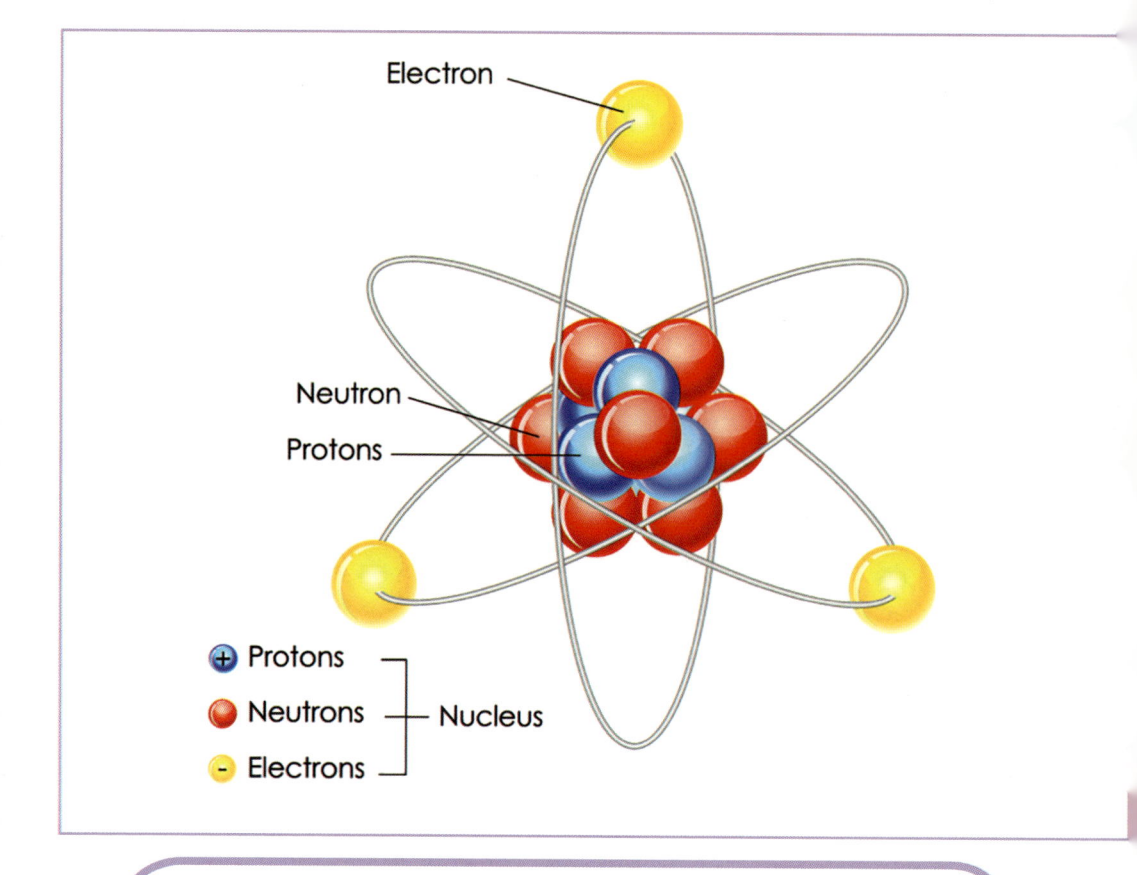

Ordinary matter is made up of atoms that consist of neutrons, protons, and electrons. Although scientists can speculate and create computer models, no one yet knows what dark matter really looks like.

and negative energy. So the very things necessary to open a wormhole are the very things that are not accurately described by Einstein's field equation.

Future scientists will make observations, develop theories, and create mathematics to describe the next level of reality. Human creativity, stimulated by these new discoveries, will build on new insights into exotic matter and the nature of gravity. Perhaps imagination and that new understanding will be the key to opening up wormhole highways across this universe and building wormhole bridges to other universes.

CHAPTER NOTES

Introduction

1. "Fastest Spacecraft Speed," Guinness World Records, accessed November 22, 2017. http://www.guinnessworldrecords.com/world-records/66135-fastest-spacecraft-speed.

Chapter 1
Wormholes in the Imagination

1. Madeleine L'Engle, *A Wrinkle in Time* (New York, NY: Farrar, Straus and Giroux, 1962).
2. *Deep Space Nine*, television program (Los Angeles, CA: Paramount Television, 1993–1999).
3. *Contact*, film, directed by Robert Zemeckis (Los Angeles, CA: Warner Brothers, 1997).
4. *Interstellar*, film, directed by Christopher Nolan (Los Angeles: Paramount Pictures, 2014).

Chapter 2
Theories of Gravity

1. Richard Gaughan, *Accidental Genius: The World's Greatest By-Chance Discoveries* (New York, NY: Metro Books, 2010), pp. 30–35.
2. Robert M. Wald, *Space, Time, and Gravity* (Chicago, IL: University of Chicago Press, 1992), pp. 13–23.
3. Norbert Straumann, *General Relativity* (New York, NY: Springer, 2013), pp. 72–78.

Chapter 3
What Is the Universe?

1. "Einstein's Pathway to Special Relativity," University of Pittsburgh, accessed November 24, 2017. http://www.pitt.edu/~jdnorton/teaching/HPS_0410/chapters_2017_Jan_1/origins_pathway/index.html.
2. Robert M. Wald, *Space, Time, and Gravity* (Chicago, IL: University of Chicago Press, 1992), pp. 31–33.
3. Jim Al-Khalili, *Black Holes, Wormholes, and Time Machines* (London, UK: IOP Publishing Ltd., 1999), pp. 28–32.
4. Norbert Straumann, *General Relativity* (New York, NY: Springer, 2013), p. 72.

Chapter 4
Scientific Reasoning

1. R. W. Hamming, "The Unreasonable Effectiveness of Mathematics," *American Mathematical Monthly* 87, no. 2 (February 1980): pp. 81–90. http://www.jstor.org/stable/2321982.
2. Raymond Tallis, "Mathematics & Reality," *Philosophy Now*, no. 102 (2014). https://philosophynow.org/issues/102/Mathematics_and_Reality.
3. James Kolata, *Elementary Cosmology: From Aristotle's Universe to the Big Bang and Beyond* (San Rafael, CA: Morgan & Claypool, 2015), pp. 15-1–15-2.

Chapter 5
Proving General Relativity

1. "Einstein Field Equations (General Relativity)," Warwick University Department of Physics, accessed November 24, 2017. https://www2.warwick.ac.uk/fac/sci/physics/intranet/pendulum/generalrelativity.

2. Frank L. Misiti Jr., "Standardizing the Language of Inquiry," *NSTA WebNews Digest*, February 1, 2001. http://www.nsta.org/publications/news/story.aspx?id=41178.

3. Simon Worrall, "The Hunt for Vulcan, the Planet That Wasn't There," *National Geographic*, November 4, 2015. https://news.nationalgeographic.com/2015/11/151104-newton-einstein-gravity-vulcan-planets-mercury-astronomy-theory-of-relativity-ngbooktalk/.

4. Estelle Asmodelle, *Tests of General Relativity: A Review* (senior thesis, University of Central Lancashire, 2017).

5. "NIST Pair of Aluminum Atomic Clocks Reveal Einstein's Relativity at a Personal Scale," NIST, September 23, 2010. https://www.nist.gov/news-events/news/2010/09/nist-pair-aluminum-atomic-clocks-reveal-einsteins-relativity-personal-scale.

6. Richard W. Pogge, "Real-World Relativity: The GPS Navigation System," Ohio State University, updated March 11, 2017,. http://www.astronomy.ohio-state.edu/~pogge/Ast162/Unit5/gps.html.

7. David Lindley, "Focus: The Weight of Light," *Phys. Rev. Focus* 16, no.1 (July 12, 2005). https://physics.aps.org/story/v16/st1.

8. "Gravitational Waves Detected 100 Years After Einstein's Prediction," Laser Interferometer Gravitational-Wave Observatory, February 11, 2016. https://www.ligo.caltech.edu/news/ligo20160211.

Chapter 6
Through the Wormhole

1. Jim Al-Khalili, *Black Holes, Wormholes, and Time Machines* (London, UK: IOP Publishing Ltd., 1999), pp. 241–245.

2. James Kolata, *Elementary Cosmology: From Aristotle's Universe to the Big Bang and Beyond* (San Rafael, CA: Morgan & Claypool, 2015), pp.13-1–14-5.

3. Albert Einstein and Nathan Rosen "The Particle Problem in the General Theory of Relativity," *Physical Review* 48, July 1, 1935.

4. Matt Visser, *Lorentzian Wormholes: From Einstein to Hawking* (Woodbury, NY: AIP Press, 1995).

5. Victoria Jaggard, "Would Astronauts Survive an Interstellar Trip Through a Wormhole?" Smithsonian.com, November 7, 2014. https://www.smithsonianmag.com/science-nature/would-astronauts-survive-interstellar-trip-through-wormhole-180953269/.

6. Kolata, p. 15-9

7. "What Is the Casimir Effect?" *Scientific American,* accessed November 24, 2017. https://www.scientificamerican.com/article/what-is-the-casimir-effec/#.

GLOSSARY

Doppler shift The change in the frequency of a signal as the source is moving. This makes a train whistle sound higher as the train is approaching and also changes the color of light for objects that travel very fast.

field equation A short but very complex equation that describes how the energy contained in matter creates a curvature in space and how a curvature in space creates energy and matter.

gedankenexperiment Usually translated as "thought experiment." A hypothetical situation that can be examined to reveal some principle of the physical world.

general relativity A mathematically complex theory that describes how matter and space interact with one another to create the structure of the universe.

gravitational waves Ripples in space-time caused by interactions between objects. They're only measurable if the objects are very heavy.

habitable Capable of supporting life. When used about another planet, it means the planet has water, oxygen, and a comfortable temperature range.

hypothesis A detailed, testable prediction about how a particular measurement will turn out. A hypothesis comes out of a more complete theory.

Kerr wormhole A rip in space-time caused by a very heavy rotating object. The object's rotation turns it into a donut shape.

law of universal gravitation A simple mathematical rule that describes how two objects, such as Earth and a person, attract one another. It is accurate in many situations, but in extreme conditions, it does not work.

mass equivalence The principle that the mass of an object reacts the same to gravitational forces as it does to other forces. Also called the weak equivalence principle.

physical model An object constructed to mimic a system being studied. An aquarium, for example, could be built as a model of a forest pond.

process The steps needed to get something done. A process can be simple or complex, but the steps will get to the goal.

space-time A consequence of special relativity. To people moving at different speeds, time and space can be measured differently, but a specific combination of time and space will always be the same.

spatial coordinates The directions needed to describe the location of an object. In three-dimensional space, those coordinates can be thought of as up and down, left and right, and forward and back.

special relativity A theory developed by Albert Einstein to deal with inconsistencies of some other important theories. Special relativity says that everyone measures the same speed of light, no matter how quickly they move.

strong equivalence principle The idea that there is no internal measurement that can be made to tell the difference between a gravitational field and acceleration at the same rate.

theory A mental model of the physical world. Theories are built on observations but also make predictions about observations that have not yet been made. When many observations support a theory, it becomes scientifically accepted.

traversable wormhole A "tear" in space-time that allows signals or matter to travel across the universe or to another universe.

unstable wormhole An opening through a rip in space-time that closes as soon as anything gets close enough to enter.

weak equivalence principle The belief that the mass acted upon by a gravitational force is the same as the mass acted upon by other forces. Also called mass equivalence.

wormhole A theoretically possible break in the fabric of space-time that could connect distant parts of the universe or even different universes. Wormholes have not yet been observed.

FURTHER READING

Books

Brezina, Corona. *Discovering Relativity.* New York, NY: Rosen, 2015.

Chown, Marcus. The *Ascent of Gravity: The Quest to Understand the Force That Explains Everything*. New York, NY: Pegasus Books, 2017.

Hilton, Lisa. *The Theory of Relativity.* New York, NY: Cavendish Square, 2016.

May, Andrew. *Albert Einstein: Scientist.* New York, NY: Cavendish Square, 2017.

Negus, James. *Black Holes Explained.* New York, NY: Enslow Publishing, 2019.

Tolish, Alexander. *Gravity Explained.* New York, NY: Enslow Publishing, 2019.

Wood, Matthew Brenden. *The Science of Science Fiction.* White River Junction, VT: Nomad Press, 2017.

Websites

Black Holes: Gravity's Relentless Pull

hubblesite.org/explore_astronomy/black_holes

Read about one way in which heavy objects distort the space around themselves: black holes.

Gravity: Making Waves

www.amnh.org/explore/science-bulletins/(watch)/astro/ documentaries/gravity-making-waves

View videos and other resources that explain the physics of gravitational waves.

Nova: Relativity and the Cosmos

www.pbslearningmedia.org/resource/phy03.sci.phys.fund. relandcosmos/relativity-and-the-cosmos

Explore the history behind Einstein's discovery of general relativity, along with an outline of the theory and its implications.

INDEX

M

mass equivalence, 35
mathematical rules, 44–46, 47
models, 31–32, 33, 44, 46,
49–51, 54

N

National Aeronautics and
Space Administration
(NASA), 16
negative energy, 66–69
Newton, Isaac, 19–20
law of universal gravitation,
20–22, 25, 54

P

Proxima Centauri, 9, 10

R

Rosen, Nathan, 62

S

science, purpose of, 30–32, 41
science fiction, 15
space, what it looks like,
36–41
space-time, 26–27, 28–29, 35,
53, 54, 56, 58, 59–60, 62,
64
spaghettification, 64

spatial coordinates, 28–29
special relativity, theory of, 26
strong equivalence principle,
35

T

theories
about, 32, 49–51
testing, 54
thought experiments, 33–36,
46–47
tight reasoning, 42–44
tunnels, 6–8, 9, 12–14

W

weak equivalence principle, 35
wormholes
defined, 6, 9, 42
early ideas about, 62
Kerr, 64
prediction of , 9, 18, 19, 42,
51, 59–60, 64–65, 66, 69
traversable, 64–65, 67
types of, 64
in works of fiction, 10–18
Wrinkle in Time, A, 10–12